3 3518 0

D0769470

JUL 16 1997

1697

11/97 - lx - 10/97
2/05 4 2/03

1691726

E
304.2   Low, Robert,
L91a   Peoples of the
        Arctic

LOS GATOS PUBLIC LIBRARY
Telephone: 408-354-6891

A fine shall be charged each day an item is kept overtime. No item will be issued to persons in arrears for fines.

Loss of, or damage to an item other than regular wear and tear, must be paid by the person to whom the book is charged.

Attention is called to the rule that items borrowed from the library must not be loaned.

For violation of these rules, the privileges of the library may be withdrawn from any person at any time.

GAYLORD F

LOS GATOS PUBLIC LIBRARY
LOS GATOS, CALIFORNIA

PEOPLES AND THEIR ENVIRONMENTS

PEOPLES OF THE ARCTIC

Robert Low

The Rosen Publishing Group's
PowerKids Press
New York

Published in 1996 by The Rosen Publishing Group, Inc.
29 East 21st Street, New York, NY 10010

Copyright © 1996 by The Rosen Publishing Group, Inc.

All rights reserved. No part of this book may be reproduced in any form without permission in writing from the publisher, except by a reviewer.

First Edition

Photo credits: Cover © P. Halley/ANAKO Editions; pp. 4, 16 © M. Poirel & C. Raoult/ANAKO Editions; p. 7 © Van Der Hilst/Gamma Liaison; pp. 8, 11 © P. Halley/ANAKO Editions; p. 12 © Wolfgang Kaehler/Gamma Liaison; p. 15 © Stein P. Aasheim/Gamma Liaison; pp. 19, 20 © Erik Sampers/Gamma Liaison.

Book Design and Layout: Kim Sonsky

Low, Robert, 1952-
    Peoples of the Arctic / Robert Low. — 1st ed.
        p.   cm. — (Peoples and their environments)
    Includes index.
    Summary: Describes life in the Arctic regions of the world and how humans have adapted to the harsh conditions there.
    ISBN 0-8239-2294-4
    1. Human geography—Juvenile literature. 2. Arctic peoples—Juvenile literature. 3. Arctic regions—Juvenile literature. [1. Arctic regions. 2. Arctic peoples. 3. Human geography.] I. Title. II. Series: Low, Robert, 1952- Peoples and their environments.
GF891.L69 1996
998—dc20   96-294
                                                                                                CIP
                                                                                                 AC

Manufactured in the United States of America

CONTENTS

LOS GATOS PUBLIC LIBRARY
LOS GATOS, CALIFORNIA

WHAT IS THE ARCTIC?

The Arctic is a very cold and beautiful place at the top of the earth. Some parts of the Arctic are so cold that the ground is always covered with snow and the water is always frozen. Other parts **thaw** (THAW) out, but only during the summer.

During the winter, there is hardly any sunlight in the Arctic. Some days there is no sunlight at all. But during the summer, the sunlight lasts from early in the morning until late at night!

◀ Much of the Arctic is frozen all year round.

Peoples Who Live in the Arctic

There are many groups of people who live in the Arctic. The Inuit, once known as Eskimos, live in the Arctic area of North America. The Sami, once called Lapps, live in the Arctic area of Europe. The Yakut and the Chukchi live in the Arctic area of Asia.

The Inuit, Sami, Yakut, and Chukchi live on different **continents** (KON-tin-nents) and speak different languages. But they do many of the same things to **survive** (ser-VIVE) in such cold weather.

The Sami live in Lapland, the Arctic area of Europe. ▶

Plants and Animals of the Arctic

Many animals that live in the Arctic, such as reindeer, polar bears, and huskies (a kind of dog), have thick fur that keeps them warm.

Whales, seals, and walruses also live in the Arctic. Their bodies are thick with blubber, a kind of fat that keeps them warm in the freezing Arctic waters. Certain types of fish live in the Arctic too.

Not many plants can survive the cold of the Arctic. But certain kinds of grass, moss, and berries grow during the summer in the places that thaw.

◀ Some Arctic people, such as the Inuit, use huskies to pull dogsleds.

Surviving the Arctic

People everywhere need food, clothing, and shelter. Because the Arctic is frozen for much of the year, people who live in the Arctic face special challenges in getting these things. They have developed ways to get these things from the **environment** (en-VIE-ron-ment) in which they live.

Arctic peoples have learned to use the resources available to survive in their cold environment, ▶ such as wearing animal furs to keep warm.

Arctic Food and Clothing

Long ago, meat and fish were the only foods many Arctic people could find. Today, in addition to meat and fish, the Inuit, Sami, Yakut, and Chukchi can also buy food grown in other places and sold in stores in the Arctic.

The people of the Arctic once made their clothes out of the skins and furs of the animals they hunted for food. Today they can buy warm clothes made of other materials, but some continue to make seal-skin boots, bear-skin pants, and reindeer-skin jackets.

◀ The Chukchi continue to wear warm clothes made from animal skins.

Hunting, Fishing, and Farming

People of the Arctic learned to get food in three ways: hunting, fishing, and farming. The Inuit once used **harpoons** (har-POONS) to catch all of their meat. Today, they also use rifles to hunt land animals such as reindeer and bears.

In the past and still today, fishermen cut holes in the ice. They drop lines with hooks on the end into the water underneath.

Some Arctic people, such as the Sami, are farmers. They raise reindeer, which eat wild grass that grows in parts of the Arctic.

Like the Sami, some Chukchi still raise reindeer. ▶

Traveling in the Arctic

In order to travel quickly over the snow- and ice-covered ground, the Inuit use dog-sleds, large sleds pulled by teams of huskies. Today, the Inuit and other Arctic peoples also use snowmobiles to get around.

To travel through the water, the Inuit build boats called **kayaks** (KY-yaks) which hold just one person, and **umiaks** (OO-mee-yaks), which hold many people. The people in these boats use paddles to drive and steer the boats through the water. Today, the Inuit use motorboats, too.

◄ Today, many people in the Arctic use snowmobiles to get around.

Building a Home

Peoples who lived in the Arctic built houses out of many different materials. The Inuit made warm, round houses called **igloos** (IG-glooz) out of snow and ice. Today, most build igloos only when they travel on long hunting trips. Some Arctic peoples made their homes out of dirt. Others, such as the Sami, and another Arctic people, the Evenk, lived in tents made of reindeer skin when traveling with their herds of reindeer. Most people living in the Arctic today make their houses out of wood brought in from other countries.

While traveling with their herds of reindeer, the Evenk build tents made of reindeer skin. ▶

FAMILIES AND COMMUNITIES

People living in the Arctic have always had to rely on each other for support and help in providing food, shelter, and clothing. Families stick close together. Inuit grandparents often live with their children and grandchildren. Grandmothers help care for their young grandchildren.

Sami families often travel and work together when they take care of their herds of reindeer.

The Yakut show their pride in their community by wearing traditional dress for a national celebration.

CHANGING TIMES

Today, many Arctic peoples live in houses made of wood, use electric lights, and have televisions. Telephone lines connect distant villages to big towns and cities. Airplanes carry mail and supplies to distant villages, and sometimes help to find reindeer herds. People shop in grocery stores and department stores. Children go to schools like yours.

Life is always changing in the Arctic.

LOS GATOS P͟ ͟RY
LOS GATOS, CALIFORNIA

Glossary

continents (KON-tin-nents) The seven largest areas of land on earth.

environment (en-VIE-ron-ment) Your surroundings.

harpoon (har-POON) A weapon like a spear, which has a sharp tip, a long pole, and a line or rope attached to it.

igloo (IG-gloo) A round house made of ice and snow.

kayak (KY-yak) A small boat that is covered except for an opening where the person paddling it can sit.

survive (ser-VIVE) To find a way to live.

thaw (THAW) To warm up and soften.

umiak (OO-mee-yak) Large boat that can hold several people.

Index

LOS GATOS PUBLIC LIBRARY
LOS GATOS, CALIFORNIA